Thank you for selecting this book as a valuable source of knowledge and inspiration. Our aim is to provide you with insights and information that will enrich your understanding and enhance your personal growth. We appreciate your decision to embark on this journey of discovery with us, and we hope that this book will exceed your expectations and leave a lasting impact on your life.

Title: Champions in Clouded Glory: Tales of the Turf

Subtitle: Versatile Horses Who Conquered the Racing World

Series: Tales of the Turf: The Legacy of White and Grey

Author: William R. Foster

Table of Contents

sun, they take on an ethereal glow. These horses, it seems, are connected to the very elements that surround them.

The symbolism of grey coats goes beyond mere aesthetics. They are like blank canvases, upon which the brushstrokes of their victories create masterpieces. Each victory, each stride, and each thundering gallop adds a new layer to the story of these champions. They are a living testament to the unpredictability and beauty of life and racing.

A Universal Fascination

The charm of grey coats transcends borders, cultures, and generations. From the verdant racecourses of the United Kingdom to the sun-soaked tracks of the United States, grey champions have left an indelible mark. Their stories resonate with fans from all walks of life, proving that the fascination with these horses is indeed universal.

In the following chapters, we will delve deep into the lives of some of the most iconic grey-coated champions in the history of horse racing. Their journeys will shed light on the multifaceted charm of grey coats, revealing the magic, the mystery, and the enduring appeal of these extraordinary horses.

As we continue our exploration of "Champions in Clouded Glory," we will celebrate the remarkable achievements, the jockeys who rode these champions to glory, and their lasting impact on the world of horse racing. The grey coats, like the clouds that grace our skies, will continue to captivate our imaginations and remind us of the enchanting beauty that exists in the world of racing.

Champions Across Disciplines

The realm of horse racing is a complex and diverse tapestry, woven with the threads of different disciplines, each with its own unique challenges and characteristics. It is within this multifaceted world that grey-coated champions have carved a niche for themselves, proving that their exceptional abilities extend beyond the confines of any single discipline. In this chapter, we embark on a journey to explore the versatility of these extraordinary horses and their triumphs in a variety of racing arenas.

Breaking the Mold

One of the most remarkable qualities of grey-coated champions is their ability to transcend the boundaries of traditional specialization. While some horses are bred and trained for specific types of races, these versatile athletes demonstrate an uncanny ability to excel across different racing disciplines. Their adaptability and athleticism are truly awe-inspiring, making them a source of fascination and admiration for racing enthusiasts.

The Classic Thoroughbred Races

Thoroughbred racing is often considered the pinnacle of the horse racing world, and it is here that grey champions have left an indelible mark. From the storied Kentucky Derby to the iconic Grand National, these horses have showcased their speed, stamina, and spirit on some of the world's most prestigious tracks. We will delve into their performances in these classic races, exploring how they faced and conquered the unique challenges posed by each.

Steeplechase and Hurdle Racing

Steeplechase and hurdle racing demand more than just speed and endurance; they require an exceptional level of agility and fearlessness. Grey-coated champions have demonstrated their prowess in these grueling events, navigating over jumps and obstacles with a grace that belies their size and strength. Their performances in steeplechase races, such as the Cheltenham Festival and the Grand National, have left spectators in awe.

Harness Racing: A Test of Endurance

In harness racing, horses pull a sulky and driver at breakneck speeds, often covering long distances. Grey champions have shown that they are not just sprinters but also possess the endurance and determination needed to succeed in this demanding discipline. The likes of Greyhound and Niatross have become legends in harness racing circles, displaying a different facet of their multifaceted talents.

International Showcases

A Glimpse into Versatility

In the world of horse racing, versatility is a prized attribute that sets certain champions apart from the rest. It's the ability to not only excel in one particular discipline but to conquer various forms of racing that truly defines a legendary equine athlete. In this chapter, we delve into the captivating world of versatility, examining how grey-coated champions have showcased their remarkable adaptability and prowess in different racing arenas.

The Power of Adaptation

Versatility in horse racing is a testament to the horse's adaptability and the skill of those who train and ride them. Grey champions, with their exceptional qualities, have time and again demonstrated their ability to thrive under diverse conditions, from sprint races on the flat to grueling tests of endurance over hurdles and fences. This adaptability is not only a reflection of their physical attributes but also their intelligence and spirit.

Conquering the Flat: Speed and Stamina

Thoroughbred racing on the flat is a world of speed and stamina, with races ranging from sprints to longer distances. Grey-coated champions have excelled in these varied contests, proving that they are not limited to one specific type of race. Their ability to accelerate with breathtaking speed in shorter events and maintain an unrelenting pace in longer ones has made them true all-rounders on the flat.

Hurdles and Steeplechases: Navigating Obstacles

Hurdles and steeplechase races add an extra layer of complexity to racing. Grey champions have displayed an uncanny ability to navigate these obstacles with grace and agility. Whether it's leaping over hurdles or tackling challenging steeplechase fences, their adaptability shines through, and their performances have left spectators in awe.

Harness Racing: Power and Precision

In the world of harness racing, grey champions have proven that they are not just about speed but also power and precision. Pulling a sulky and driver at high speeds over long distances demands a unique set of skills. Their strength and tenacity have made them stars in harness racing events, proving that their versatility extends beyond the traditional realms of horse racing.

International Dominance

The global stage provides an even more challenging arena for these versatile champions. Racing in different countries, climates, and conditions, they have showcased their adaptability and the universality of their appeal. Winning races like the Dubai World Cup or the Breeders'

Cup Classic, where horses from various backgrounds and regions compete, is a testament to their versatility on the world stage.

Records and Achievements

As we explore the versatility of grey-coated champions, we will dive deep into the records and achievements that have solidified their place in the annals of horse racing history. Their performances across disciplines have shattered records, set new standards, and garnered adoration from fans around the world.

The Heart of Versatility: The Horse's Spirit

While physical attributes are undoubtedly a critical component of versatility, it is the spirit and heart of the horse that truly make them exceptional. The willingness to push beyond their comfort zone, adapt to new challenges, and strive for excellence is a hallmark of these champions. It's a testament to the profound bond between horse and rider that enables them to excel in different forms of racing.

In the chapters that follow, we will delve into the stories of specific grey-coated champions who have showcased their extraordinary versatility and left an indelible mark on the racing world. Their journeys provide a unique glimpse into the multifaceted nature of horse racing, where adaptability and resilience are celebrated. These grey champions, with their unwavering spirit, are living proof that greatness knows no bounds, and the world of horse racing is richer for their presence.

Chapter 1: Desert Orchid (United Kingdom, 1979-2006), Grey

Desert Orchid's Early Career and Promise

In the hallowed halls of horse racing history, few names shine as brightly as Desert Orchid. This magnificent grey steed emerged onto the racing scene in the late 20th century, capturing the hearts of racing enthusiasts around the world. In this chapter, we take a journey into the early years of Desert Orchid, where promise and potential began to weave a tale of greatness.

The Birth of a Grey Legend

Born in the bucolic setting of Ireland in 1979, Desert Orchid, often affectionately referred to as "Dessie," was a colt whose future was destined for greatness. Even in his earliest days, his distinctive grey coat set him apart. Grey horses, as we've come to know, often possess an otherworldly charm, and this young colt was no exception.

From the moment he took his first shaky steps on the lush Irish pastures, there was an air of promise about him. The lineage of great horses flowed in his veins, and it was evident that he was destined to make a significant mark on the world of racing. His early years were marked by growth, training, and a gradual unveiling of his incredible potential.

The Training Ground: Preparing for Stardom

Desert Orchid's journey to greatness began in the hands of expert trainers and handlers. From his early days of breaking and schooling to the intensive training sessions that would shape his racing career, Dessie displayed a remarkable aptitude for learning and a spirit that refused to be dimmed.

It's during these formative years that the promise of Desert Orchid truly started to shine. His trainers saw in him a unique combination of qualities: speed, stamina, a love for the chase, and an undying spirit. These early training sessions were the crucible in which his talents were honed, preparing him for the challenges that lay ahead.

First Steps on the Racecourse

Every champion's career has a starting point, and for Desert Orchid, it was his maiden race. The anticipation was palpable as the grey colt was led onto the racecourse, his striking coat gleaming in the sunlight. It was a moment of promise, where potential met reality, and Dessie did not disappoint. He showed an exceptional burst of speed and determination, marking the beginning of a career that would become the stuff of legends.

In these early races, Desert Orchid's promise was undeniable. He displayed an affinity for the racetrack, an understanding of the game, and an eagerness to compete. Each victory and near miss served as a stepping stone, propelling him toward a future where he would etch his name in the annals of racing history.

The Unseen Challenges

While Desert Orchid's early career showed immense promise, it was not without its challenges. The life of a racehorse is a demanding one, with rigorous training schedules, the pressure to perform, and the inherent risks of injury. Dessie, however, displayed not only physical prowess but also an enduring spirit that carried him through the tough times.

His early years also bore witness to the incredible bond that formed between him and his jockey, Colin Brown. The partnership between horse and rider is a crucial element in a racehorse's success, and Desert Orchid's relationship with Brown was to become one of the defining factors in his career.

In the chapters that follow, we will delve deeper into Desert Orchid's remarkable journey, from his earliest triumphs to his iconic performances that would solidify his status as one of the greatest racehorses of all time. His early career was a promise, and it was a promise that he would more than fulfill, leaving an indelible mark on the world of horse racing.

The Stunning 1989 Cheltenham Gold Cup Victory

In the annals of British horse racing, the Cheltenham Gold Cup stands as one of the most prestigious and revered events. It is a race that has witnessed the triumphs of legends, and in 1989, it bore witness to a moment of racing history that would etch Desert Orchid's name in gold. In this chapter, we relive the exhilarating journey that led to his unforgettable victory in the 1989 Cheltenham Gold Cup.

The Road to Cheltenham

As the racing world turned its attention to the 1989 Cheltenham Gold Cup, Desert Orchid had already established himself as a force to be reckoned with. His early career had been marked by promising performances, and he had a growing fan base that adored him for his spirited runs and distinctive grey coat.

The path to Cheltenham was paved with trials and triumphs. Dessie's preparation for the Gold Cup was meticulous and comprehensive. His trainers, David Elsworth and Colin Brown, knew that they had a special horse on their hands, and they were determined to ensure he was in peak condition for the biggest race of his life.

The Field of Champions

The Cheltenham Gold Cup is known for attracting the best of the best, both in terms of horses and jockeys. The

1989 edition was no different. Desert Orchid faced formidable opponents, each with their own impressive records and credentials. The lineup was a veritable who's who of the racing world, and the stage was set for a battle of epic proportions.

As the competitors paraded onto the hallowed Cheltenham turf, the excitement in the air was palpable. The crowd, too, was electrified, as they waited with bated breath to witness a race that would become the stuff of legends.

The Race of a Lifetime

The Cheltenham Gold Cup is a test of not only a horse's physical abilities but also its mental fortitude. The grueling race covers a distance of three miles and two and a half furlongs, featuring a series of challenging fences that demand precision and courage. It is a race that separates the exceptional from the merely good.

The 1989 Gold Cup was a rollercoaster of emotions. Desert Orchid's supporters watched with a mix of hope and trepidation as he navigated the course, displaying his signature daring jumps and remarkable speed. The race was marked by fierce competition, with horses pushing their limits, but it was clear that Dessie was in a league of his own that day.

The Iconic Fences

Cheltenham is known for its iconic fences, and in the 1989 Gold Cup, Desert Orchid's performance over these obstacles was nothing short of breathtaking. His jumps were not just athletic; they were the leaps of a champion in the making. It was at these pivotal moments that he showcased the blend of skill and heart that set him apart.

As Dessie cleared the final fence and raced toward the finish line, the crowd erupted in a deafening roar. It was a moment of pure racing magic, as the grey champion, with his distinctive coat glistening in the Cheltenham sun, crossed the line to a thunderous ovation.

A Triumph of Spirit

The 1989 Cheltenham Gold Cup victory was more than just a win; it was a triumph of spirit. Desert Orchid's performance on that historic day encapsulated everything that makes racing great. It was a testament to the enduring bond between horse and jockey, as Colin Brown expertly guided him to victory.

The victory also resonated with fans on a profound level. Desert Orchid's story was not just about winning races; it was about defying the odds, overcoming challenges, and capturing the hearts of a nation. His victory was celebrated not only by racing enthusiasts but by anyone who appreciated the power of determination and the beauty of a dream realized.

In the chapters that follow, we will continue to unravel the remarkable journey of Desert Orchid, exploring the impact of his 1989 Cheltenham Gold Cup victory and the enduring legacy of this grey champion. His triumph was more than a race; it was a moment that would forever be etched in the history of horse racing, a moment of stunning victory that would stand the test of time.

His Remarkable Win in the King George VI Chase

Desert Orchid's legacy as a true icon of horse racing was built upon a series of extraordinary victories, and one of the most memorable of these was his remarkable triumph in the King George VI Chase. In this chapter, we will delve into the lead-up, the race itself, and the enduring significance of Desert Orchid's win in this prestigious event.

The King George VI Chase: A Storied History

The King George VI Chase is one of the jewels in the crown of British National Hunt racing. Held annually on Boxing Day at Kempton Park Racecourse, it draws the best chasers from the UK and beyond. The racecourse, with its undulating terrain and challenging fences, provides the perfect stage for a true test of stamina, skill, and bravery.

As Desert Orchid's career progressed, the King George became a fixture on his racing calendar. His early attempts at the race did not yield victory, but they provided invaluable experience that would shape his future attempts.

A Unique Connection: Desert Orchid and His Jockey, Simon Sherwood

In horse racing, the relationship between jockey and horse is often the linchpin of success. For Desert Orchid, the bond with his jockey, Simon Sherwood, was a special one.

The trust and understanding between the two were instrumental in the grey champion's accomplishments.

Sherwood, who had been aboard Dessie for many of his career-defining races, shared a unique connection with the horse. Their partnership was marked by mutual respect, and it was a testament to the skill of both horse and jockey that they were able to achieve greatness together.

The 1986 King George VI Chase: A Glimpse of Glory

Desert Orchid's journey to his first King George VI Chase victory in 1986 was not without its challenges. As the race unfolded, it became clear that the grey champion was poised for greatness. His jumps were precise, his speed relentless, and his spirit unyielding.

In a race where the competition was fierce, it was Dessie who displayed the heart of a champion. The moment he cleared the final fence and powered down the Kempton Park straight, the crowd erupted in a thunderous cheer. Desert Orchid had secured his place in the annals of racing history with a victory that would be remembered for generations to come.

The 1988 King George VI Chase: A Repeat Performance

Desert Orchid's win in 1986 was not a one-off; it was a preview of what was to come. In 1988, he returned to the

King George VI Chase with the intention of defending his title. The racing world watched with bated breath to see if he could replicate the magic of his previous victory.

Once again, Dessie dazzled the spectators and silenced the doubters. His performance was a display of pure class and tenacity, as he surged ahead in the final furlongs to secure his second King George VI Chase victory. It was a feat that only the greatest of horses could achieve, and Dessie had firmly established himself as one of the greatest.

The Legacy of Desert Orchid's King George Victories

Desert Orchid's consecutive victories in the King George VI Chase were more than just remarkable wins; they were a testament to the enduring spirit of racing. His success in these races served as an inspiration to both those within the racing community and those far beyond it.

The legacy of these wins is not just a series of trophies but a reminder of the beauty and power of the sport. Desert Orchid's victories transcended the track; they became moments of collective celebration, moments when the magic of racing was captured in its purest form.

In the chapters that follow, we will continue our exploration of Desert Orchid's remarkable career, his enduring popularity, and the impact of his King George VI Chase victories. These wins were more than just races; they were moments of sheer brilliance, etching Desert Orchid's name into the heart of British horse racing history.

The Enduring Popularity of a Beloved Grey Champion

Desert Orchid's legacy extends far beyond his victories on the racetrack. His distinctive grey coat and charismatic personality captured the hearts of racing enthusiasts and the wider public alike. In this chapter, we delve into the enduring popularity of Desert Orchid and how he became a beloved figure in the world of horse racing.

The Grey Marvel: A Distinctive Presence

From his early days in the racing world, Desert Orchid's grey coat made him a standout figure. In a sport often characterized by the traditional chestnut and bay coats of Thoroughbreds, Dessie's unique coloring was an immediate attention-grabber. His striking appearance, resembling a silver meteor streaking across the track, earned him the nickname "The Grey Marvel."

But it wasn't just his coat that set him apart. It was his captivating personality, a blend of intelligence, spirit, and playfulness. He wasn't just a horse; he was a character, and the public quickly fell in love with his exuberance and charm.

Connecting with the Public

Desert Orchid's appeal extended beyond the racing community. He became a household name in the United Kingdom, known even to those who had never set foot on a racecourse. His accessibility and relatability were unique among elite racehorses. The public found a connection with him, and it was a connection that would endure for years to come.

One of the reasons for this deep connection was his remarkable consistency on the racetrack. Desert Orchid was not just a one-hit wonder; he repeatedly delivered thrilling performances, making him a horse to cheer for with each appearance. He was a champion who raced for the people, and they responded with unwavering support.

The Power of Victories

Desert Orchid's victories, especially in prestigious events like the King George VI Chase, solidified his status as a true champion. These wins were not just personal triumphs; they were moments of collective celebration. When Dessie crossed the finish line, the roar of the crowd was a testament to the joy he brought to so many.

His 1986 and 1988 King George VI Chase victories were particularly iconic. The scenes of him galloping to victory with his grey coat gleaming in the winter sun are etched in the memories of racing enthusiasts. These wins didn't just endear him to racing fans; they turned him into a national treasure.

A Horse of the People

Desert Orchid's impact extended beyond the racetrack. He became a symbol of hope, perseverance, and the enduring spirit of competition. His story was a source of inspiration, demonstrating that even in the face of challenges and setbacks, greatness could be achieved.

As Dessie continued to race and excel, his fan base grew. The public followed his every move, and his victories became moments of collective celebration. It was a reminder that horse racing was not just a sport; it was a shared experience that could unite people from all walks of life.

Retirement and Legacy

While every great champion eventually retires, Desert Orchid's popularity didn't wane. His retirement from racing marked the end of one chapter but the beginning of another in his enduring legacy. He remained a beloved figure, making appearances at various events and becoming a symbol of the timeless charm of horse racing.

Dessie's legacy continues to inspire new generations of racing enthusiasts. His story is a reminder that greatness is not confined to the racetrack but can transcend time and place. Desert Orchid, "The Grey Marvel," remains eternally etched in the hearts of those who had the privilege of witnessing his greatness, and his enduring popularity is a testament to the profound impact he made on the world of horse racing.

Chapter 2: Silver Charm (United States, 1994-2014), Grey

Silver Charm's Journey from His Early Races to Stardom

The story of Silver Charm, the charismatic grey champion, is a testament to the indomitable spirit of a true Thoroughbred. From his humble beginnings to his meteoric rise to stardom, this chapter takes us through the remarkable journey of a horse who captured the hearts of racing enthusiasts in the United States and beyond.

The Early Days: A Promising Colt

Silver Charm's journey began in 1994 when he was foaled in Pennsylvania, USA. From his earliest days, it was evident that he possessed the qualities of a future champion. His conformation, lineage, and natural athleticism set him apart from the rest, and it wasn't long before he found himself on the path to a career in horse racing.

As a young colt, Silver Charm underwent training that would prepare him for a life on the racetrack. His trainers recognized his potential and nurtured his talents, carefully guiding him through the early stages of his racing career.

Debut on the Track

Silver Charm made his racing debut as a two-year-old, marking the beginning of a journey that would take him to some of the most prestigious racetracks in the United States. In these early races, he displayed glimpses of his immense talent, capturing the attention of racing enthusiasts and industry professionals.

His early races were a mix of triumphs and learning experiences. Silver Charm was in the process of honing his racing skills, and each race, whether a victory or a defeat, contributed to his development as a racehorse.

Triple Crown Dreams: The Kentucky Derby

The pinnacle of American horse racing is the Triple Crown, a series of three races that every owner, trainer, and jockey dreams of winning. Silver Charm's journey to stardom reached its zenith in the spring of 1997 when he entered the Kentucky Derby, the first leg of the Triple Crown.

The Kentucky Derby is renowned for its rich history and intense competition. Silver Charm's victory in this prestigious event marked a turning point in his career. It was a race that showcased his speed, stamina, and sheer determination, establishing him as a legitimate contender for the elusive Triple Crown.

The Preakness Stakes: A Gritty Triumph

Following his Kentucky Derby win, Silver Charm faced the challenge of the Preakness Stakes. This grueling race is the second leg of the Triple Crown and is known for its demanding distance and competitive field.

Silver Charm's victory in the Preakness Stakes was a testament to his grit and resilience. The race showcased his ability to face adversity and triumph in a hard-fought battle, setting the stage for the ultimate test of the Triple Crown.

The Belmont Stakes: A Heartbreaking Defeat

The final leg of the Triple Crown, the Belmont Stakes, is known for its challenging distance. Silver Charm entered this race with the hopes of becoming the first Triple Crown winner in nearly two decades. The nation watched with bated breath as he raced towards history.

In a heart-wrenching finish, Silver Charm narrowly lost the Belmont Stakes, missing the Triple Crown by a mere half-length. While the defeat was a disappointment, it did not diminish the champion's stature. His journey to the brink of Triple Crown glory was a testament to his talent and tenacity.

Enduring Legacy

Silver Charm's journey from his early races to stardom was marked by a combination of raw talent, dedication, and the unwavering support of his team. His impact on American horse racing extended beyond the track. He became a symbol of hope and resilience, inspiring those who followed his remarkable career.

In the chapters that follow, we will delve deeper into the life and legacy of Silver Charm, exploring his international success, the Dubai World Cup triumph, and the timeless appeal of this versatile grey champion. His journey from humble beginnings to stardom serves as a shining example of the enduring allure of Thoroughbred horse racing.

The 1997 Kentucky Derby and Preakness Stakes Wins

In 1997, Silver Charm embarked on a journey that would etch his name in the annals of American horse racing history. His victories in the Kentucky Derby and Preakness Stakes, the first two legs of the Triple Crown, are a testament to his exceptional talent and determination. In this chapter, we relive these momentous victories and the impact they had on the world of Thoroughbred racing.

The Kentucky Derby: The Run for the Roses

The Kentucky Derby, often referred to as the "Run for the Roses," is the first leg of the American Triple Crown. It's a race that has captivated the imagination of horse racing enthusiasts for generations. In 1997, Silver Charm, under the guidance of jockey Gary Stevens, entered the hallowed grounds of Churchill Downs with dreams of Derby glory.

The 1997 Kentucky Derby was a fiercely competitive event, featuring a field of talented three-year-old colts. Silver Charm's performance in this iconic race showcased his exceptional speed and stamina. As he thundered down the homestretch, it became evident that he was a colt destined for greatness.

Silver Charm's victory in the Kentucky Derby was not just a triumph; it was a moment of racing history. It marked the culmination of years of training, dedication, and hard work by his team. The crowd erupted in cheers as he crossed the finish line, his grey coat shimmering in the Kentucky sun. He had not only won a race but had earned a place in the hearts of racing fans.

The Preakness Stakes: A Gritty Battle

Following his Kentucky Derby victory, Silver Charm set his sights on the Preakness Stakes, the second leg of the Triple Crown. The Preakness is known for its shorter distance and competitive field, and it often tests a horse's speed and resilience to the fullest.

The 1997 Preakness Stakes would prove to be a thrilling duel. Silver Charm faced formidable opponents, including Free House and Captain Bodgit. As the horses thundered down the homestretch, Silver Charm demonstrated his sheer determination and heart, edging out his rivals to secure the second leg of the Triple Crown.

His victory in the Preakness Stakes showcased Silver Charm's versatility. He could not only triumph in the Kentucky Derby, a race that tested stamina, but also prevail in the Preakness, a contest that demanded pure speed. It was a demonstration of his well-rounded racing abilities and a testament to the partnership between horse and jockey.

The Brink of Triple Crown Glory

Silver Charm's victories in the Kentucky Derby and Preakness Stakes set the stage for a historic bid for the Triple Crown. He had captured the hearts of racing enthusiasts and had the nation's attention as he prepared for the Belmont Stakes, the third and final leg of the Triple Crown.

The prospect of a Triple Crown victory had eluded horse racing for nearly two decades, and Silver Charm was on the brink of making history. The anticipation was palpable, and the nation watched with bated breath as he raced toward Belmont Park, where his date with destiny awaited.

In the chapters that follow, we will explore Silver Charm's pursuit of the elusive Triple Crown and the impact of his Kentucky Derby and Preakness Stakes victories. These races were not just moments of triumph but also stages where a grey champion's journey to stardom was illuminated, leaving an indelible mark on the world of Thoroughbred racing.

His International Success, Including the Dubai World Cup

Silver Charm's journey from a rising star in American horse racing to international success was marked by his exceptional talent, versatility, and indomitable spirit. In this chapter, we explore his remarkable foray onto the global stage, with a particular focus on his historic victory in the Dubai World Cup.

A Star in the Making

Silver Charm's triumphs in the Kentucky Derby and Preakness Stakes had already cemented his status as a beloved American racing icon. His consistency and remarkable racing ability captured the imagination of racing enthusiasts, but it was his versatility that would soon carry him beyond American shores.

As discussions about his future unfolded, the prospect of international competition arose. Silver Charm's trainers and connections saw an opportunity to showcase his talent on a global stage, and the decision was made to enter the world of international racing.

The Global Stage: Dubai World Cup

The Dubai World Cup is one of the world's richest and most prestigious horse races. Held at the opulent Meydan Racecourse in Dubai, it draws an international field of the best Thoroughbreds from around the world. It is a race that carries not only substantial financial rewards but also a legacy of greatness.

In 1998, Silver Charm made the journey from the United States to Dubai, ready to take on the world. The anticipation was palpable as the grey champion prepared to enter the starting gates. Racing enthusiasts from around the world eagerly awaited his performance in the Dubai World Cup, a race that would be a defining moment in his international career.

A Grueling Test of Stamina

The Dubai World Cup is known for its demanding distance of 2,000 meters (about 1.24 miles) on the dirt track. It is a race that tests a horse's stamina, speed, and adaptability. Silver Charm's versatility had already been demonstrated in his American victories, and now he faced the challenge of acclimating to a new racing environment.

The 1998 Dubai World Cup was a fiercely competitive event, with top horses from various countries vying for glory. Silver Charm's performance in this race would not only test his physical prowess but also his mental fortitude. As the starting gates opened, he surged forward, displaying the spirit that had endeared him to fans around the world.

A Historic Victory

Silver Charm's run in the Dubai World Cup was nothing short of spectacular. The race, often described as a test of the world's best horses, showcased the grey champion's adaptability and competitive spirit. He navigated the demanding distance with precision and surged ahead in the homestretch.

As he crossed the finish line, the crowd erupted in cheers. Silver Charm had not only won the Dubai World Cup; he had become the first American-trained horse to claim victory in this prestigious event. His win was a moment of racing history, a testament to his extraordinary ability and a demonstration of American racing prowess on the global stage.

Legacy and Impact

Silver Charm's victory in the Dubai World Cup was more than just a win; it was a moment that resonated with racing enthusiasts worldwide. His performance showcased the universality of racing excellence and the enduring appeal of Thoroughbred horse racing.

In the chapters that follow, we will continue to explore Silver Charm's international success and his legacy in the world of horse racing. His journey from American racing sensation to global icon is a testament to his extraordinary talent and the enduring allure of the sport. Silver Charm's story is a celebration of the power of racing to unite people across borders and leave an indelible mark on the world of sports.

The Timeless Appeal of a Versatile Grey Horse

Silver Charm, the charismatic grey champion, possessed qualities that made him not only a beloved figure in horse racing but also a symbol of enduring appeal. In this chapter, we explore the unique and timeless charm of grey horses, focusing on Silver Charm's versatility, grace, and the reasons for his enduring popularity.

The Enigmatic Allure of Grey Horses

Grey horses have a unique and timeless allure in the world of horse racing. Their coats, ranging from light silver to dark dapple, set them apart from the more common bay and chestnut horses. The sight of a grey horse on the racetrack is often a mesmerizing and ethereal experience, capturing the imagination of racing enthusiasts and the public.

Silver Charm's distinctive grey coat was a source of fascination. It was a coat that seemed to shimmer in the sunlight, earning him the affectionate nickname "The Grey Flash." His appearance on the racetrack was an event in itself, and it showcased the enigmatic and captivating allure of grey horses.

Versatility and Adaptability

Silver Charm's versatility was one of his most remarkable qualities. He excelled in a variety of racing conditions, from the dirt tracks of Kentucky to the turf of Dubai. This adaptability was not unique to Silver Charm alone but is a characteristic often associated with grey horses.

Grey horses have demonstrated their ability to compete in various racing disciplines. They have won classic races on the flat and hurdles over jumps, showcasing their agility, speed, and endurance. Silver Charm's victories in different racing environments exemplified the versatility of grey horses, adding to their timeless appeal.

The Symbolism of Grey Coats

Grey horses have often been associated with qualities such as wisdom, elegance, and nobility. The symbolism of grey coats goes beyond their physical appearance and delves into the realm of myth and legend. In many cultures, grey horses have been revered and considered special.

Silver Charm's grey coat embodied not only his physical attributes but also the symbolism attached to grey horses. He was more than just a racehorse; he was a representation of beauty, grace, and the enduring spirit of competition.

Fan Connection and Loyalty

The enduring popularity of grey horses like Silver Charm is also tied to the deep connections they form with their fans. Racing enthusiasts often develop strong attachments to these horses, and these connections can last a lifetime.

Silver Charm's charismatic personality and spirited performances forged a bond with fans that went beyond the racetrack. People from all walks of life felt a sense of ownership and pride in his achievements. His wins were celebrated collectively, and his losses were felt deeply.

The Grey Champions of Racing History

Silver Charm was not the only grey champion to capture the hearts of racing enthusiasts. Throughout the history of horse racing, grey horses have left their mark on the sport. Horses like Desert Orchid, Arkle, and Kauto Star have become legendary figures in their own right, each adding to the timeless appeal of grey horses.

The stories of these grey champions are a testament to the enduring allure of grey coats. They have become part of racing folklore, their legacies passed down from one generation of racing enthusiasts to the next.

In the chapters that follow, we will continue to explore the legacy of Silver Charm and the impact of grey horses on the world of horse racing. Their timeless appeal is a reminder that in the ever-evolving world of sports, some things remain constant and eternally captivating.

Chapter 3: Dahlia (France, 1970-2001), Grey Dahlia's Origins and Early Career in France

Dahlia, the iconic grey mare, left an indelible mark on the world of horse racing. Her journey from humble beginnings to international stardom is a testament to her exceptional talent and the unwavering dedication of her team. In this chapter, we delve into Dahlia's origins and her early career in France, where her remarkable story began.

Birth of a Star: Foaling of Dahlia

Dahlia's story begins on April 2, 1970, when she was foaled in France. Her birth came with the promise of greatness, as she hailed from a lineage of distinguished racing heritage. Her sire, Vaguely Noble, was a champion racehorse, and her dam, Charming Alibi, brought her own set of prestigious bloodlines to the table.

Dahlia's distinctive grey coat, a signature of her ancestry, set her apart from her contemporaries from the very beginning. It was a coat that would become a symbol of grace and elegance, characteristics that would define her throughout her racing career.

Early Days of Training

Dahlia's early training days were marked by the careful guidance of her trainers, primarily Maurice Zilber. Her talent and willingness to learn were evident from the outset. It wasn't long before she made her racing debut in France, commencing a career that would capture the imagination of racing enthusiasts worldwide.

Her initial races served as a foundation for her future successes. Dahlia's progress on the racetrack demonstrated her racing acumen and versatility. Her performances, even in her early days, hinted at the extraordinary potential that lay within her.

Rising Star in France

As Dahlia continued to race in her native France, she quickly earned a reputation as a rising star. Her victories in notable races such as the Prix de l'Arc de Triomphe and the Prix Saint-Alary were early indicators of her immense talent. These wins not only established her as a formidable force in French racing but also piqued the interest of the international racing community.

Dahlia's racing style was characterized by her grace and determination. Her ability to accelerate when needed and her tenacity in the closing stages of a race made her a favorite among both fans and jockeys. These qualities, which would become her hallmark, were already evident in her early career.

International Recognition

Dahlia's early career success in France laid the foundation for her international recognition. Her remarkable performances piqued the interest of racing enthusiasts and professionals in other countries, setting the stage for her future endeavors on a global scale.

As she prepared to leave French shores for new challenges, Dahlia had already left an indelible mark on the racing world. Her reputation as a gifted grey mare with a heart full of determination and a coat that seemed to shimmer in the French sun had transcended borders.

The Early Chapters of a Remarkable Journey

Dahlia's early career in France was just the beginning of a story that would continue to unfold on an international stage. Her performances in France showcased her potential, while her distinctive grey coat and exceptional racing ability endeared her to fans.

In the chapters that follow, we will explore Dahlia's journey beyond France, her dominance in international races, and the lasting legacy of this exceptional grey mare. Her story is not just one of racing success but also a testament to the enduring allure of Thoroughbred horse racing and the transcendent power of champions like Dahlia.

Her International Triumphs, Including the Washington, D.C. International Stakes

Dahlia's journey from her early career in France to international stardom was marked by her exceptional talent and versatility. In this chapter, we delve into her triumphs on the global stage, with a particular focus on her iconic victory in the Washington, D.C. International Stakes, a race that would define her legacy as one of the greatest turf mares in racing history.

The Washington, D.C. International Stakes: A Prestigious Event

The Washington, D.C. International Stakes, held at Laurel Park in Maryland, USA, was one of the most prestigious turf races in the world. It attracted a field of top-class horses from various countries, creating an international spectacle that celebrated the spirit of competition.

Dahlia's entry into this historic race was met with great anticipation. Her reputation as an exceptional grey mare with a penchant for turf racing had already transcended borders. The 1973 edition of the Washington, D.C. International Stakes would be a defining moment in her career.

Facing International Rivals

The international nature of the Washington, D.C. International Stakes meant that Dahlia would face formidable opponents from around the world. Horses from the United States, Europe, and other racing powerhouses converged on Laurel Park, creating a truly global racing showcase.

Dahlia's ability to adapt to different racing conditions had already been demonstrated in her early career. Her versatility was a significant advantage as she prepared to take on competitors from diverse backgrounds, each with their own unique racing styles and strategies.

Dahlia's Victory in the 1973 Washington, D.C. International Stakes

The 1973 Washington, D.C. International Stakes was a race for the ages. As the horses thundered down the turf course, Dahlia displayed her exceptional talent and competitive spirit. Her jockey, Lester Piggott, guided her with precision, showcasing the partnership between horse and rider.

In a thrilling finish, Dahlia surged ahead, overtaking her rivals to claim victory in the Washington, D.C. International Stakes. Her win was not just a triumph; it was a statement of her dominance on the turf. Racing enthusiasts around the world celebrated her achievement, recognizing her as a true international racing sensation.

Global Recognition and Legacy

Dahlia's victory in the Washington, D.C. International Stakes elevated her status to that of a global racing icon. She became a symbol of excellence, capturing the hearts of fans and professionals alike. Her performance in this historic race resonated with those who appreciated the timeless beauty of turf racing.

Dahlia's international triumphs, including the Washington, D.C. International Stakes, served as a testament to the enduring appeal of Thoroughbred horse racing. Her legacy extended beyond the racetrack, inspiring future generations of racing enthusiasts and showcasing the international nature of the sport.

Dahlia's Impact on Racing

Dahlia's international success, particularly her victory in the Washington, D.C. International Stakes, left an indelible mark on the world of horse racing. She not only demonstrated the transcendent power of a champion but also highlighted the global reach of the sport.

In the chapters that follow, we will continue to explore Dahlia's remarkable career, her dominance in prestigious races, and her lasting impact on the world of Thoroughbred horse racing. Her story is a testament to the enduring allure of the sport and the ability of exceptional athletes like Dahlia to capture the hearts of racing enthusiasts across borders.

Her Dominance in Races like the King George VI and Queen Elizabeth Stakes

Dahlia's racing career was marked by a series of extraordinary victories, and her dominance in prestigious races, including the King George VI and Queen Elizabeth Stakes, established her as one of the greatest turf mares in horse racing history. In this chapter, we delve into Dahlia's remarkable performances in these iconic races and the impact they had on her legacy.

The King George VI and Queen Elizabeth Stakes: A Classic Event

The King George VI and Queen Elizabeth Stakes, held at Ascot Racecourse in England, is one of the most prestigious and revered races in the world of Thoroughbred horse racing. It is a race that attracts top-class horses from various countries, creating a stage where greatness is achieved and legacies are established.

Dahlia's entry into the King George VI and Queen Elizabeth Stakes was met with immense anticipation. The race represented an opportunity to prove her mettle on the international stage, facing off against the best turf horses in the world.

Dahlia's Triumph in the 1973 King George VI and Queen Elizabeth Stakes

The 1973 edition of the King George VI and Queen Elizabeth Stakes would be remembered as a defining moment in Dahlia's career. The race featured a formidable field of competitors, including some of the most renowned turf horses of the era. Dahlia's jockey, Lester Piggott, guided her with precision, knowing that the race would be a true test of her ability.

As the horses thundered down the Ascot turf, Dahlia demonstrated her extraordinary talent. Her ability to accelerate when needed and her unwavering determination propelled her to a remarkable victory. She crossed the finish line, greeted by cheers from racing enthusiasts who recognized her as a true champion.

A Rivalry for the Ages: Dahlia vs. Brigadier Gerard

One of the most memorable aspects of Dahlia's victories in the King George VI and Queen Elizabeth Stakes was her rivalry with another turf legend, Brigadier Gerard. The battles between these two exceptional horses captivated the racing world and turned each encounter into a highly anticipated event.

The duels between Dahlia and Brigadier Gerard showcased the spirit of competition and the sheer determination of both horses. These races were a testament to the quality of racing during that era and left an indelible mark on the history of the sport.

Global Recognition and Legacy

Dahlia's dominance in races like the King George VI and Queen Elizabeth Stakes not only established her as a turf queen but also elevated her status to that of a global racing sensation. She captured the hearts of racing enthusiasts worldwide, transcending borders with her performances.

Her victories in prestigious events such as the King George VI and Queen Elizabeth Stakes left an enduring legacy. They served as a testament to the enduring appeal of turf racing and the power of exceptional racehorses to create moments that resonate with fans and professionals alike.

Dahlia's Impact on Racing

Dahlia's dominance in races like the King George VI and Queen Elizabeth Stakes was a testament to her exceptional talent and the enduring allure of Thoroughbred horse racing. Her legacy extends beyond her victories and serves as a reminder of the timeless beauty and excitement of the sport.

In the chapters that follow, we will continue to explore Dahlia's remarkable career, her international success, and the profound impact she had on the world of horse racing. Her story is not just one of racing excellence but also a celebration of the enduring legacy of champions like Dahlia, who continue to inspire new generations of racing enthusiasts.

The Enduring Legacy of a Graceful Grey Mare

Dahlia, the remarkable grey mare, left an indelible legacy in the world of horse racing. Her impact extended far beyond the racetrack, and her story continues to inspire racing enthusiasts and professionals alike. In this chapter, we explore the lasting influence and enduring legacy of this graceful grey mare.

The Iconic Grey Mare

Dahlia's iconic grey coat set her apart from her contemporaries. It wasn't just her racing ability that captured the hearts of fans but also her physical beauty and ethereal presence on the racetrack. Her grey coat, which ranged from a shimmering silver to a dappled hue, became her signature, earning her the nickname "The Grey Angel."

Grey horses have always held a special place in the world of horse racing. They are often seen as enigmatic and captivating, and Dahlia embodied these qualities. Her presence on the racetrack was not just about racing; it was a celebration of her unique appearance and the enduring charm of grey horses.

Versatility and Adaptability

Dahlia's versatility was one of her most remarkable traits. She excelled on both turf and dirt tracks, proving herself in a variety of racing conditions. Her adaptability made her a formidable competitor and endeared her to fans who admired her ability to conquer different challenges.

Grey horses, in general, have often displayed the same versatility. They have won classic flat races, hurdle races, and steeplechases, showcasing their ability to adapt to various disciplines. Dahlia's success added to the reputation of grey horses as being not only beautiful but also exceptionally talented and adaptable.

A Global Sensation

Dahlia's racing career took her from France to the United States and other countries, earning her recognition as a global sensation. Her performances on international stages, including victories in prestigious races like the Washington, D.C. International Stakes and the King George VI and Queen Elizabeth Stakes, showcased her as a true ambassador of the sport.

Dahlia's impact transcended borders, uniting racing enthusiasts around the world in appreciation of her remarkable talent and the enduring appeal of horse racing. Her legacy served as a reminder of the international nature of the sport and the power of exceptional racehorses to connect people across cultures.

A Fierce Rivalry and Sporting Spirit

Dahlia's rivalry with Brigadier Gerard, one of the greatest horses in British racing history, is etched in racing lore. Their duels captivated audiences and elevated the sport to new heights. The fierce but respectful competition between these two exceptional horses highlighted the sporting spirit of horse racing.

The legacy of their rivalry remains a symbol of what makes horse racing special – the pursuit of excellence, the thrill of competition, and the respect that exists between rivals. Dahlia's part in this rivalry made her a symbol of true sportsmanship.

Continued Inspiration

Dahlia's enduring legacy goes beyond her lifetime. Her story continues to inspire those in the racing industry and fans of the sport. Her performances, her elegance, and her ability to capture the imagination of people endure through stories, photographs, and videos that serve as a testament to her greatness.

In the chapters that follow, we will explore the profound impact Dahlia had on the world of horse racing, her post-racing career, and the ways in which she continues to be celebrated and remembered. Her legacy is a testament to the enduring allure of Thoroughbred horse racing and the power of exceptional athletes like Dahlia to leave an indelible mark on the hearts of those who admire them.

Chapter 4: Albino (Argentina, 1915-1940), Albino (pure white coat)

Albino's Unique Coat Color and Early Races in Argentina

Albino, the extraordinary pure white horse, captured the imagination of horse racing enthusiasts not only through his exceptional racing prowess but also due to his striking and rare coat color. In this chapter, we delve into the uniqueness of Albino's coat color and his early racing career in Argentina, where his remarkable story began.

The Purity of White: Albino's Coat Color

Albino's pure white coat was an extraordinary rarity in the world of horse racing. His coat lacked any pigmentation, giving him an almost ethereal appearance on the racetrack. The pristine whiteness of his coat, often described as "albino" due to the absence of color, set him apart from other horses and made him an instant sensation.

The genetic factors that contribute to a pure white coat in horses are a subject of fascination for both scientists and enthusiasts. Albino's coat, a result of a genetic anomaly, was a source of wonder and amazement, and it would become one of his defining features throughout his career.

Early Days of Training and Development

Albino's journey in the world of horse racing began in his native Argentina. His early training and development under the guidance of skilled trainers marked the foundation of his racing career. His handlers recognized his potential not only as a unique-looking horse but also as a horse with remarkable athleticism.

Albino's early races in Argentina provided glimpses of his exceptional talent. He demonstrated speed, stamina, and an unyielding spirit that set the stage for his future achievements. His handlers, jockeys, and supporters saw in him the potential for greatness.

A Rising Star on the Argentine Racing Scene

As Albino continued to develop and gain experience, he quickly rose to prominence on the Argentine racing scene. His performances in local races and on well-known tracks such as the Hipódromo Argentino de Palermo showcased his racing acumen and the unique charm of his pure white appearance.

The Argentine racing community and fans recognized Albino not only as a talented racehorse but also as a symbol of rarity and excellence. His victories in races were celebrated not only for their sporting significance but also for the representation of a remarkable and unique horse.

The Unique Challenges of Albino's Coat

Albino's pure white coat presented unique challenges beyond the racetrack. The absence of pigmentation made him more susceptible to certain skin conditions and required special care. His handlers had to take extra precautions to protect his skin from the sun's intensity and other environmental factors.

The challenges posed by Albino's coat were met with dedication and care, ensuring that he remained in peak condition throughout his racing career. His unique physical traits added to the complexity of his story and the admiration of those who followed his career.

Albino's Impact Beyond Argentina

While Albino's early racing career was centered in Argentina, his unique coat and exceptional racing abilities soon drew attention from the global racing community. Racing enthusiasts and professionals from other countries were captivated by the rare and beautiful white horse from South America.

Albino's impact transcended national borders, and he would soon embark on an international journey that would further elevate his status as a global racing sensation.

In the chapters that follow, we will explore Albino's international success, his role as a symbol of excellence and rarity, and the enduring memory of this extraordinary white horse. His story is not just one of racing achievement but also a celebration of the remarkable and unexpected in the world of horse racing.

His Prestigious Wins, Including the Gran Premio Nacional

Albino, the remarkable pure white horse, captured the hearts of racing enthusiasts not only for his unique coat color but also for his exceptional racing abilities. In this chapter, we delve into Albino's prestigious wins, with a special focus on his triumphant performance in the Gran Premio Nacional, a race that showcased his true greatness and solidified his status as an iconic racing figure.

The Gran Premio Nacional: A Landmark Race

The Gran Premio Nacional, often referred to as the Argentine Derby, is one of the most prestigious and challenging races in South American horse racing. Held annually at the Hipódromo Argentino de Palermo in Buenos Aires, it draws the best three-year-old Thoroughbreds from Argentina and neighboring countries.

Albino's entry into the Gran Premio Nacional was met with great anticipation. The race represented not only a chance to prove his mettle but also to solidify his place in racing history. Winning the Argentine Derby was a dream held by trainers, jockeys, and horse owners alike, and Albino was about to embark on a journey that would capture the imagination of the racing world.

A Unique Challenge: Racing as the White Wonder

Albino's pure white coat was not just a distinctive feature; it also posed unique challenges on the racetrack. The absence of pigmentation made him more sensitive to environmental factors, particularly the sun. His handlers had to take special precautions to ensure he remained comfortable and healthy, adding a layer of complexity to his racing preparations.

Despite these challenges, Albino's racing career had demonstrated his remarkable talent and adaptability. The Gran Premio Nacional would be the ultimate test of his abilities, as it required both speed and stamina over a grueling distance.

The Triumph of Albino in the Argentine Derby

The day of the Gran Premio Nacional arrived, and Albino stood at the starting gate, his pure white coat shining in the Argentine sun. The race was a test of endurance, covering a challenging distance that separated the exceptional from the extraordinary.

Albino's jockey, guided by the horse's handlers and trainers, executed a race strategy that showcased his exceptional ability. As the race unfolded, Albino's talent and heart came to the forefront. He surged ahead in the homestretch, leaving his competitors in his wake. The sight of the white wonder crossing the finish line first was met with jubilation from the crowd.

Albino's victory in the Gran Premio Nacional was not just a win; it was a statement of his dominance in Argentine racing. He had conquered one of the most challenging races in South America, solidifying his status as a racing legend and a symbol of excellence.

The Legacy of Albino's Gran Premio Nacional Win

Albino's victory in the Gran Premio Nacional left a lasting legacy in the world of horse racing. His triumph was celebrated not only for its sporting significance but also for the symbolism it carried. Albino had overcome challenges, both on and off the racetrack, to achieve greatness.

His win in the Argentine Derby added to his reputation as a rare and exceptional horse. It served as an inspiration to those who admired his unique qualities and his remarkable racing prowess.

In the chapters that follow, we will continue to explore Albino's extraordinary career, his role as a symbol of excellence and rarity, and the enduring memory of this extraordinary white horse. His story is a testament to the power of exceptional racehorses to inspire and captivate the world of horse racing.

Albino's Role as a Symbol of Excellence and Rarity

Albino, the pure white horse from Argentina, was not just a remarkable racehorse; he became a symbol of excellence and rarity in the world of horse racing. In this chapter, we delve into the significance of Albino's unique presence, his impact on the sport, and how he embodied the qualities of a symbol.

The Rare and Exquisite White Wonder

Albino's pure white coat made him an exceptional rarity in the equine world. While horses come in a multitude of coat colors and patterns, true albino horses are exceptionally uncommon. His coat, devoid of pigmentation, set him apart from his peers and captured the imagination of those who saw him. Albino's presence was a testament to the diversity and wonder of the equine world.

A Testament to Exceptionalism

Albino's unique appearance was not the only reason he became a symbol of excellence. His racing career demonstrated his exceptional talent, tenacity, and adaptability. He faced unique challenges due to his coat color, yet he consistently excelled on the racetrack.

The combination of his rare physical traits and racing prowess made him an exceptional racehorse. Albino embodied the idea that excellence knows no boundaries, whether in the realm of appearance or athletic ability.

Inspirational to Racing Enthusiasts

Albino's story served as an inspiration to racing enthusiasts around the world. His journey from Argentina to international recognition showcased the possibilities within horse racing. He proved that a horse's potential should not be limited by their appearance, and that extraordinary qualities can be found in unexpected places.

For those who followed Albino's career, he became a symbol of hope and encouragement. He encouraged fans to celebrate the individuality of each horse and recognize the potential for greatness, even in the most unique circumstances.

A Unifying Presence

Albino's presence in the racing world was unifying. His unique coat color transcended national borders, captivating racing enthusiasts from different countries. He became a unifying figure in a sport that often features competition between nations.

His appearances on the international racing stage brought people together in celebration of his extraordinary talent and exceptional beauty. Albino served as a reminder that the love for horse racing knows no boundaries and that exceptional horses are appreciated by all.

The Legacy of Rarity

Albino's role as a symbol of excellence and rarity did not end with his retirement from racing. His legacy continued to inspire those within the racing industry and beyond. He remained a symbol of what can be achieved when exceptional individuals are celebrated and encouraged.

In the chapters that follow, we will explore Albino's post-racing life, the ways in which he continued to inspire, and the enduring memory of this extraordinary white horse. His story is a testament to the power of exceptional racehorses to symbolize excellence, rarity, and the unifying spirit of horse racing.

The Enduring Memory of an Extraordinary White Horse

Albino, the extraordinary pure white horse, left a profound impact on the world of horse racing and the hearts of those who admired him. His legacy continues to inspire and evoke a sense of wonder, transcending time and place. In this chapter, we explore the enduring memory of Albino, celebrating his contributions to the sport and his lasting influence.

Capturing the Imagination

Albino's unique appearance and exceptional racing abilities made him a horse of distinction. His pure white coat was not only a rarity but a captivating spectacle that drew people to the racetrack. Albino's presence captured the imagination of those who witnessed him, and he became a living legend.

The memory of Albino, with his glistening white coat against the backdrop of the racetrack, remains etched in the minds of those fortunate enough to have seen him in action. Even for those who only heard of him, his image is one of beauty, rarity, and excellence.

Celebrating Exceptional Racing Moments

Albino's racing career was marked by exceptional moments of triumph and glory. His victories in prestigious races, including the Gran Premio Nacional, are celebrated as landmarks in the sport. These moments of excellence serve as a reminder of what can be achieved through dedication, talent, and determination.

The memory of Albino's victories in these races continues to be a source of inspiration to racing enthusiasts and professionals. They stand as a testament to the heights that horse racing can reach, and the enduring allure of exceptional racehorses.

A Symbol of Rarity and Beauty

Albino's pure white coat made him not only a symbol of rarity but also a symbol of extraordinary beauty. Horses have long been admired for their grace and majesty, and Albino exemplified these qualities in a unique way. His legacy extends to all horses, celebrating their individuality and the wonder of the equine world.

The memory of Albino is a celebration of the diverse and exquisite beauty found in the world of horses. It serves as a reminder that each horse is a work of art in its own right, with its unique coat colors and patterns.

Influence on Future Generations

Albino's memory has not faded with time; instead, it continues to influence future generations of racing enthusiasts. Those who have heard of his remarkable story are inspired by his journey, his unique qualities, and his ability to overcome challenges.

His legacy encourages individuals to appreciate the exceptional qualities of racehorses, whether in their appearance or their performance. The enduring memory of Albino reminds us of the power of exceptional horses to capture the hearts and minds of those who love horse racing.

Preserving the Legacy

Efforts to preserve the legacy of Albino continue today. Through written records, photographs, and documentaries, his story is kept alive for future generations to discover and appreciate. These endeavors ensure that the memory of Albino remains a source of inspiration and admiration.

In the chapters that follow, we will explore Albino's post-racing life, his ongoing influence on the world of horse racing, and the ways in which he is celebrated and remembered. His story is not just one of racing achievement but also a testament to the enduring allure of Thoroughbred horse racing and the lasting impact of extraordinary athletes like Albino.

Chapter 5: Versatility Beyond Bounds
Exploring the Remarkable Versatility of Grey-Coated Champions

Grey-coated champions in the world of horse racing have left an indelible mark on the sport, not only for their stunning appearance but also for their exceptional versatility. In this chapter, we delve into the unique qualities that define grey-coated champions and explore how they have excelled in various racing disciplines, showcasing their adaptability and skill.

The Allure of Grey-Coated Horses

Grey-coated horses have always held a special place in the hearts of racing enthusiasts. Their unique coloration, ranging from striking silver to dappled grey, sets them apart from the more common chestnuts and bays. Grey-coated champions often command attention with their captivating presence on the racetrack.

The allure of grey-coated horses is not limited to their appearance; it extends to their versatility and racing prowess. These horses, while known for their striking coats, are celebrated for their ability to excel in different racing disciplines, from flat racing to jumps and steeplechases.

Mastering Multiple Disciplines

Grey-coated champions have proven time and again that their talents extend beyond a single racing discipline. They have showcased their adaptability by mastering a wide range of racing types, each with its unique challenges and demands.

Flat Racing: Speed and Elegance

In the world of flat racing, where speed and endurance are paramount, grey-coated champions have shone as exemplars of grace and agility. Their sleek bodies and athletic builds make them well-suited to sprinting down the straight tracks, leaving their competitors in their wake.

The ability of grey-coated horses to conquer flat racing is a testament to their versatility and competitiveness. They have demonstrated that their striking appearance is matched by their racing prowess.

Jumps and Hurdles: Leaping to Victory

Grey-coated champions have also made their mark in jumps and hurdle racing. These disciplines require a different set of skills, including the ability to navigate obstacles and maintain a steady pace. Grey-coated horses have shown that they are up to the challenge, leaping to victory and showcasing their adaptability.

Their success in jumps and hurdle races is a testament to their intelligence and dexterity. Grey-coated champions have displayed an innate understanding of the sport, whether it involves clearing obstacles on a steeplechase course or tackling hurdles on the track.

Steeplechasing: Courage and Endurance

Steeplechasing, a discipline known for its demanding and grueling nature, has seen grey-coated champions excel. These races test a horse's courage, endurance, and jumping ability, and grey-coated champions have consistently demonstrated their mettle.

Grey-coated horses' ability to conquer steeplechases reflects their tenacity and spirit. They are willing to face the challenges presented by this demanding discipline and emerge as champions.

The Grey-Coated Icons

Throughout the history of horse racing, grey-coated champions have left their mark as iconic figures. Horses like Desert Orchid, Silver Charm, and Dahlia, known for their exceptional versatility, have captured the hearts of racing enthusiasts and earned their place in the annals of the sport.

The legacy of grey-coated champions extends beyond their physical traits; it encompasses their ability to excel in a variety of racing disciplines. Their enduring appeal lies in their adaptability and the thrill they bring to the world of horse racing.

In the chapters that follow, we will further explore the characteristics that make grey-coated champions stand out and the challenges and advantages they encounter in their quest for excellence. Grey-coated champions continue to inspire and leave an indelible mark on the sport they grace with their presence.

The Challenges and Advantages of Being a Multi-Discipline Champion

Grey-coated champions who excel in multiple racing disciplines face a unique set of challenges and enjoy distinct advantages that set them apart in the world of horse racing. In this chapter, we explore what it means to be a multi-discipline champion and how these exceptional horses navigate the complexities of mastering different racing types.

The Demands of Multi-Discipline Excellence

Becoming a multi-discipline champion is no small feat. Horses that excel in various racing disciplines must possess a range of qualities and skills, including speed, agility, endurance, and adaptability. Meeting the demands of multiple disciplines is a testament to their exceptional athleticism.

Physical Versatility: The Advantage of Grey-Coated Champions

Grey-coated champions, with their striking and unique appearance, often display a remarkable degree of physical versatility. Their sleek bodies, well-defined musculature, and athletic builds make them well-suited to different types of racing. The advantages of being grey-coated are not limited to aesthetics but extend to the physical attributes that enable these horses to thrive in various racing disciplines.

Adaptability: Navigating Different Race Conditions

One of the primary challenges faced by multi-discipline champions is adapting to the diverse race conditions of each discipline. Flat racing, jumps and hurdles, and steeplechases each present their own unique challenges, from navigating sharp turns to leaping over obstacles. Grey-coated champions must quickly adjust to the requirements of each discipline.

Consistency: Maintaining Peak Performance

Consistency is a hallmark of champions, and grey-coated horses who excel in multiple disciplines are no exception. Maintaining peak performance across different types of races requires meticulous training and conditioning. These horses must be able to shift their focus from one discipline to another without a drop in performance.

The Weight of Expectations: Meeting High Standards

Grey-coated champions who succeed in multiple disciplines often face high expectations. Their exceptional talent and versatility set the bar for their performance. Fans, owners, and trainers anticipate victories and records, which can be a source of pressure on these horses.

Managing the Rigors of Training

The training regimens for horses who compete in multiple disciplines can be grueling. These champions must be prepared physically and mentally for the demands of different types of races. The training schedule, exercise routines, and the need for rest must be carefully balanced to ensure they are in top condition for every race.

The Joy of Variety: A Horse's Perspective

While grey-coated champions may face challenges in their multi-discipline journey, they also enjoy a unique advantage – variety. Horses, like humans, can experience boredom and fatigue when subjected to the same routine. Competing in different types of races can provide mental stimulation and excitement, making their racing careers more fulfilling.

The Legacy of Multi-Discipline Champions

The multi-discipline champions, like Desert Orchid and Silver Charm, are celebrated not only for their versatility but also for the indelible legacy they leave in the world of horse racing. Their remarkable achievements inspire admiration and respect, serving as a reminder of the boundless potential of exceptional racehorses.

In the chapters that follow, we will delve deeper into the characteristics that make grey-coated champions stand out, the partnerships they form with their jockeys, and the records and achievements that shape their legacy. Grey-coated champions continue to captivate the racing world, their stories a testament to the enduring allure of Thoroughbred horse racing.

The Characteristics That Make These Horses Stand Out

Grey-coated champions in the world of horse racing possess a unique set of characteristics that set them apart and contribute to their remarkable success. In this chapter, we explore the qualities that define grey-coated champions and make them stand out in the competitive world of horse racing.

Exceptional Physical Beauty

One of the most immediate and striking qualities of grey-coated champions is their exceptional physical beauty. These horses, with their glistening silver or dappled grey coats, are a spectacle to behold on the racetrack. Their beauty is not just skin deep; it extends to their overall conformation, making them stand out even in a field of talented racehorses.

Striking Presence

Grey-coated champions have a magnetic presence that captures the attention of spectators and racing enthusiasts. Whether in the paddock before a race or galloping down the homestretch, their unique appearance commands admiration. Their striking presence adds an element of drama and excitement to the sport.

Versatility and Adaptability

Grey-coated champions are known for their versatility and adaptability. They have the ability to excel in various racing disciplines, from flat racing to jumps and steeplechases. This adaptability showcases their intelligence, athleticism, and willingness to take on different challenges.

Exceptional Racing Prowess

Beyond their appearance, grey-coated champions are celebrated for their exceptional racing abilities. They possess the speed, stamina, and determination required to win races at the highest level. Their performances on the racetrack consistently demonstrate their prowess, earning them accolades and the admiration of fans.

Tenacity and Heart

Grey-coated champions often display remarkable tenacity and heart, which are qualities that endear them to fans. They are willing to fight to the finish, even in the face of adversity. This tenacity and heart, combined with their racing abilities, make for thrilling performances and exciting races.

The Ability to Capture Hearts

Grey-coated champions have an uncanny ability to capture the hearts and imaginations of those who follow horse racing. Their unique appearance, combined with their outstanding performances, creates a deep emotional connection with fans. These horses become beloved figures in the sport, their stories told and retold as part of racing lore.

Resilience and Longevity

Many grey-coated champions enjoy long and successful racing careers, often competing at a high level for years. Their resilience and longevity are admirable qualities, as they continue to perform at their best even as they age. Their enduring careers are a testament to their physical soundness and mental fortitude.

The Power of Symbolism

Grey-coated champions often symbolize excellence, rarity, and the unifying spirit of horse racing. Their stories extend beyond their individual achievements; they represent the idea that exceptional qualities can be found in unexpected places and that the love for horse racing transcends national borders.

In the chapters that follow, we will delve deeper into the connections these champions form with their jockeys, their records and achievements, and the lasting impact they have on the world of horse racing. Grey-coated champions continue to inspire and capture the hearts of those who appreciate the exceptional qualities they bring to the sport.

Chapter 6: The Bonds of Horse and Rider Celebrating the Jockeys Who Rode These Versatile Champions to Victory

The success of grey-coated champions in the world of horse racing is not solely a result of their exceptional abilities. Behind every triumphant race, there is a jockey who forms an essential partnership with the horse. In this chapter, we celebrate the jockeys who rode these versatile champions to victory, exploring their skills, connections, and the profound impact they had on the horses' careers.

The Vital Role of Jockeys

Jockeys are the unsung heroes of horse racing, playing a pivotal role in a horse's performance. Their expertise in race tactics, riding skills, and understanding of the horses' strengths and weaknesses are instrumental in achieving victory. For grey-coated champions, finding the right jockey can make all the difference.

The Jockey-Horse Connection

The bond between a jockey and a horse is a unique and often profound relationship. Jockeys spend countless hours with their equine partners, learning their personalities, preferences, and racing styles. This deep connection allows jockeys to bring out the best in their horses and guide them to victory.

Understanding the Versatility

Jockeys who ride grey-coated champions in various disciplines possess a keen understanding of the versatility required. They adapt their riding techniques and strategies to the demands of flat racing, jumps and hurdles, or steeplechases. Their ability to navigate different race types is a testament to their skill and adaptability.

Strategies and Racecraft

Successful jockeys are masters of racecraft, developing strategies that leverage the strengths of their horses while capitalizing on the weaknesses of competitors. In multi-discipline racing, these strategies must be flexible, with jockeys making quick decisions during the race to ensure victory.

The Patience and Dedication of Jockeys

The journey of a jockey can be one of great patience and dedication. They work tirelessly to maintain their physical fitness, hone their riding skills, and study the intricacies of the sport. This dedication is especially evident when they partner with grey-coated champions, who often excel in a variety of disciplines.

The Joy of Victory

For jockeys who guide grey-coated champions to victory, the joy of winning is immeasurable. The thrill of crossing the finish line first, the roar of the crowd, and the knowledge that they played a significant role in the horse's success are deeply rewarding. These moments of victory become cherished memories in a jockey's career.

The Legacy of Jockey-Horse Partnerships

The partnerships between jockeys and grey-coated champions often leave a lasting legacy in the world of horse racing. The synergy between horse and rider, their shared successes, and the admiration of fans all contribute to a sense of history and tradition. These partnerships are celebrated not only for their individual achievements but for the profound impact they have on the sport.

In the chapters that follow, we will delve deeper into the records and achievements of grey-coated champions, their lasting influence on horse racing, and the enduring fascination with these extraordinary athletes. The bond between horse and rider is at the heart of the sport, and jockeys who guided grey-coated champions to victory are a testament to the power of partnership in the world of Thoroughbred horse racing.

The Connections and Partnerships That Fueled Their Success

Behind every successful grey-coated champion in horse racing, there is a dynamic partnership between the horse and its rider. In this chapter, we delve into the connections and partnerships that played a pivotal role in fueling the success of these versatile champions. These relationships are not just about racing; they are a profound bond that brings out the best in both horse and jockey.

A Relationship Built on Trust

The foundation of the horse-rider partnership is trust. Grey-coated champions place their trust in their jockeys, knowing that they will be guided safely and strategically through the race. In turn, jockeys trust their horses to perform at their best and respond to their cues. This mutual trust is the bedrock of their connection.

Understanding Each Other's Strengths and Weaknesses

Jockeys who have formed deep connections with grey-coated champions understand the strengths and weaknesses of their horses. They know when to push their horses to excel and when to conserve energy. This intimate knowledge allows them to make split-second decisions during races.

The Role of Communication

Communication between horse and rider is often nonverbal but incredibly effective. Jockeys communicate with their horses through subtle shifts in weight, rein contact, and leg pressure. Grey-coated champions, in turn, respond to these cues with precision. This communication is a testament to the subtlety and nuance of their connection.

Shared Experiences and Milestones

Grey-coated champions and their jockeys share a journey filled with milestones and experiences. The thrill of winning a major race, the challenges faced along the way, and the trials they overcome all contribute to a shared history. These shared experiences deepen their bond.

Mental and Emotional Connection

The connection between grey-coated champions and their jockeys goes beyond the physical. There is a mental and emotional bond that develops over time. Jockeys understand the moods and behaviors of their horses, and horses respond to the emotional cues of their riders. This emotional connection is a source of motivation and resilience.

A Source of Inspiration

The strong connections between grey-coated champions and their jockeys serve as a source of inspiration to others in the world of horse racing. These partnerships remind racing enthusiasts and professionals of the power of mutual trust and understanding. They highlight the extraordinary achievements that can be unlocked when horse and rider work together seamlessly.

Long-Lasting Friendships

The relationships between grey-coated champions and their jockeys often extend beyond the racetrack. Long-lasting friendships are formed, with jockeys having a deep affection for the horses they have ridden to victory. Many retired champions find loving homes with their former jockeys, continuing their bond even in retirement.

The Legacy of Partnership

The partnerships between grey-coated champions and their jockeys leave a lasting legacy in the world of horse racing. These connections are celebrated not only for their individual achievements but for the profound impact they have on the sport. Their stories are a testament to the power of collaboration, trust, and a deep understanding between horse and rider.

In the chapters that follow, we will explore the records and achievements of grey-coated champions, the impact of their stories on fans, race enthusiasts, and the racing world, and the timeless fascination with these extraordinary athletes. The connections and partnerships at the heart of horse racing continue to inspire and captivate those who appreciate the enduring allure of Thoroughbred horse racing.

The Triumphs and Challenges Faced by Both Horse and Rider

The journey of a grey-coated champion and their jockey is marked by a series of triumphs and challenges, each contributing to the rich tapestry of their partnership. In this chapter, we explore the victories and obstacles that both horse and rider encounter on their path to success, highlighting the remarkable resilience and determination that define their shared journey.

Triumphs in the Face of Adversity

Triumph in horse racing often comes after overcoming adversity. Both horse and rider must navigate obstacles, setbacks, and fierce competition to achieve victory. The moments of triumph are a testament to their unwavering dedication and resilience.

The Sweet Taste of Victory

The joy of crossing the finish line first, the thrill of a major win, and the roar of the crowd are moments that define the career of a jockey and the legacy of a grey-coated champion. These victories are not only a source of pride but also a validation of the hard work and commitment they have invested.

Redefining Limits and Records

Grey-coated champions, often celebrated for their versatility, have a unique opportunity to redefine the limits of their racing discipline. They challenge records, push boundaries, and inspire future generations of horses and jockeys to aim higher. Their achievements set new benchmarks for excellence.

The Challenges of Injury and Recovery

In the world of horse racing, injuries are an unfortunate reality. Both horse and rider may face injuries that disrupt their careers. Overcoming these physical challenges and embarking on a journey of recovery requires resilience, patience, and the unwavering support of the racing community.

Facing the Demands of Competition

Competition in horse racing can be fierce. Grey-coated champions often find themselves pitted against other exceptional racehorses, each with their own set of skills and achievements. The challenges posed by such competition test their mettle and drive them to reach new heights.

The Role of Strategy and Adaptability

Jockeys must constantly adapt their strategies based on race conditions, the behavior of their horse, and the actions of competitors. Grey-coated champions demonstrate their adaptability by following their jockey's cues and executing strategies to perfection.

The Emotional Rollercoaster

The journey of both horse and rider in the world of horse racing is marked by an emotional rollercoaster. The highs of victory and the lows of defeat are part of the sport. Navigating these emotions and maintaining focus in the face of both triumph and disappointment is a significant challenge.

The Bond That Sustains

Throughout the trials and triumphs, the bond between grey-coated champions and their jockeys remains a constant source of strength. The deep connection, trust, and shared experiences provide the foundation on which they build their resilience.

The Triumphs Beyond the Racetrack

The success of grey-coated champions and their jockeys often extends beyond the racetrack. Their victories inspire racing enthusiasts, capturing the imaginations of fans and leaving a lasting impact on the racing world. The triumphs of these partnerships are celebrated not only for their individual achievements but for the enduring fascination they create.

In the chapters that follow, we will explore the records and achievements of grey-coated champions, their influence on fans, race enthusiasts, and the racing world, and the timeless charm and allure of these extraordinary athletes. The journey of both horse and rider is a testament to the unbreakable spirit of Thoroughbred horse racing.

Chapter 7: A Legacy of Excellence
The Records and Achievements of These
Multifaceted Champions

Grey-coated champions in horse racing leave behind a trail of remarkable records and achievements that serve as a testament to their extraordinary talent and versatility. In this chapter, we delve into the incredible feats and milestones that define the legacy of these multifaceted champions, highlighting their impact on the sport.

Breaking Records and Setting Benchmarks

Grey-coated champions often make history by breaking records and setting new benchmarks in their respective racing disciplines. Whether it's a record-breaking time in a flat race, a series of consecutive wins, or a dominant performance in steeplechasing, their achievements capture the imagination of racing enthusiasts.

Triumphs in Prestigious Races

Many grey-coated champions have secured victories in some of the most prestigious and challenging races in the world. Their triumphs in events like the Kentucky Derby, Cheltenham Gold Cup, Dubai World Cup, and Grand National Steeplechase have solidified their status as iconic figures in horse racing.

Consistency and Longevity

Consistency in performance and longevity in a racing career are remarkable achievements in their own right. Grey-coated champions often compete at a high level for several years, maintaining their form and competitiveness even as they age. Their enduring careers are a testament to their soundness and resilience.

Versatility in Multi-Discipline Success

One of the most exceptional achievements of grey-coated champions is their versatility in excelling across multiple racing disciplines. They may conquer flat racing, jumps and hurdles, and steeplechases, displaying their adaptability and skill. Their ability to perform well in diverse racing types sets them apart from their peers.

International Acclaim

Grey-coated champions frequently gain international acclaim, showcasing their talent on a global stage. Their success in international races, such as the Dubai World Cup or the Washington, D.C. International Stakes, brings recognition to their abilities beyond their home turf. Their international victories symbolize the unifying power of horse racing.

Earning a Place in Racing History

The records and achievements of grey-coated champions secure their place in the annals of horse racing history. Their names become synonymous with excellence and are celebrated by racing enthusiasts for generations. Their stories are retold as part of the sport's rich tapestry.

The Impact on Future Generations

The records and achievements of grey-coated champions serve as an inspiration to future generations of racehorses and jockeys. They demonstrate what is possible when exceptional talent is coupled with dedication, training, and a deep connection between horse and rider. These champions set the bar high for aspiring athletes in the sport.

A Lasting Influence on the Sport

The legacy of grey-coated champions extends beyond their individual records and achievements. They leave a lasting influence on the world of horse racing, shaping the way the sport is perceived and celebrated. Their impact is felt in the continued fascination and admiration they inspire.

In the chapters that follow, we will explore the enduring charm and allure of grey-coated champions, the stories of their multifaceted careers, and the timeless resonance of their legacy. The records and achievements of these remarkable athletes are a testament to the enduring allure of Thoroughbred horse racing.

The Impact of Their Stories on Fans, Race Enthusiasts, and the Racing World

The tales of grey-coated champions transcend the racetrack, leaving an indelible mark on fans, race enthusiasts, and the broader world of horse racing. In this chapter, we explore the profound impact these stories have had on the hearts and minds of those who follow the sport, as well as the lasting influence on the racing community.

Inspiration for Aspiring Jockeys and Trainers

The stories of grey-coated champions inspire the next generation of jockeys and trainers. Young and aspiring athletes look to these extraordinary horses and their dedicated jockeys as role models. Their stories serve as a testament to what can be achieved with hard work, talent, and unwavering commitment to the sport.

Fandom and Adoration

Grey-coated champions often amass dedicated fan followings. These fans, often referred to as "superfans," passionately support their favorite horses, attending races, collecting memorabilia, and even traveling long distances to witness the champions in action. The horses become iconic figures with fan clubs and dedicated social media followings.

A Source of Emotional Connection

The stories of grey-coated champions create a deep emotional connection between fans and the sport. These horses become more than athletes; they are symbols of hope, perseverance, and the enduring spirit of horse racing. Their triumphs and challenges resonate with the personal journeys of those who follow their careers.

Community and Tradition

Grey-coated champions often play a central role in the sense of community and tradition within the racing world. Their stories are shared among fans and professionals alike, creating a sense of belonging and camaraderie. These champions become part of the traditions that make horse racing a cherished and timeless sport.

Educational Value

The stories of grey-coated champions offer valuable lessons in the history, science, and culture of horse racing. They provide educational material for schools and universities, contributing to a deeper understanding of the sport. These champions are celebrated not only for their athletic prowess but also for their contribution to the broader educational landscape.

Economic Impact

The popularity of grey-coated champions extends beyond the racetrack, contributing to the economic aspects of the racing industry. They drive attendance at race meetings, boost television ratings, and stimulate the sale of merchandise. The economic impact of these champions ripples through the racing world.

Promotion of Grey-Coated Horses

The success stories of grey-coated champions promote the value of horses with unique coat colors. This can lead to increased interest in breeding, racing, and owning grey-coated horses. Their stories serve as a reminder that exceptional talent can be found in horses of all colors.

Racing World Relevance

Grey-coated champions continue to make headlines and remain relevant in the racing world, even long after their retirement. They are often invited as special guests at racing events, where they receive standing ovations and adoration from fans. Their presence keeps the legacy of Thoroughbred horse racing alive.

The Enduring Allure of Thoroughbred Racing

The impact of grey-coated champions on fans, race enthusiasts, and the racing world at large is a testament to the enduring allure of Thoroughbred horse racing. Their stories capture the essence of the sport, where dreams, triumphs, and the indomitable spirit of athletes come together to create an unforgettable legacy.

In the chapters that follow, we will explore the timeless charm and allure of grey-coated champions, their multifaceted careers, and the enduring resonance of their legacy. The stories of these remarkable athletes continue to captivate the hearts and minds of those who appreciate the beauty and excitement of horse racing.

The Lasting Fascination with 'Champions in Clouded Glory'

The book 'Champions in Clouded Glory' is not merely a collection of stories about grey-coated champions in horse racing; it is a testament to the timeless allure and fascination these remarkable athletes continue to hold in the hearts and minds of enthusiasts. In this final chapter, we explore the enduring charm of the book itself, examining the reasons it continues to captivate readers and maintain its relevance in the world of sports literature.

A Window into Racing History

'Champions in Clouded Glory' serves as a window into the rich history of horse racing. The book chronicles the journeys of grey-coated champions from different eras, providing readers with insights into the evolution of the sport, the changing techniques and technologies, and the enduring passion of those involved in the racing world.

The Power of Narrative

The narratives of grey-coated champions, as presented in the book, go beyond the statistics and race results. They weave a compelling story of triumph, adversity, resilience, and the deep bond between horse and rider. The power of storytelling makes the book a source of inspiration and fascination.

Continued Influence on Racing Enthusiasts

'Champions in Clouded Glory' continues to influence racing enthusiasts by introducing them to the stories of horses they may not have previously known. The book sparks curiosity and encourages readers to explore the legacies of these champions further, deepening their appreciation for the sport.

Educational Value

The book serves as an educational resource for both newcomers to the sport and experienced racing professionals. It offers insights into the training, racing, and breeding of grey-coated champions, enriching readers' understanding of horse racing. Its educational value ensures its enduring relevance.

A Source of Nostalgia

For those who have followed horse racing for years, 'Champions in Clouded Glory' evokes a sense of nostalgia. It allows readers to revisit the eras when these champions raced and to relive the excitement and emotions of their victories. The book becomes a cherished link to the past.

Engagement and Conversation

The book fosters engagement and conversation among racing enthusiasts. Readers discuss their favorite stories, debate the merits of different champions, and share their personal connections to the sport. 'Champions in Clouded Glory' becomes a catalyst for a sense of community among fans.

A Gift for Future Generations

The book also serves as a gift for future generations. As readers share their love of horse racing with their children and grandchildren, they pass on the stories of grey-coated champions, ensuring that their legacy endures and that new generations will continue to be fascinated by the sport.

The Timeless Allure of Grey-Coated Champions

Ultimately, 'Champions in Clouded Glory' is a celebration of the timeless allure of grey-coated champions in horse racing. Their unique qualities, remarkable achievements, and the deep connections they form with their jockeys make for a narrative that transcends time and continues to inspire and captivate readers.

In closing, the book 'Champions in Clouded Glory' stands as a testament to the enduring charm and fascination of Thoroughbred horse racing. Its stories of grey-coated champions, their partnerships with jockeys, and their lasting impact on the sport ensure that the book itself remains a cherished piece of literature for all who appreciate the beauty and excitement of horse racing.

Conclusion
The Timeless Charm of Versatile Champions

In the grand tapestry of Thoroughbred horse racing, the enduring allure of versatile champions, particularly those with grey coats, remains a captivating and timeless phenomenon. In this final chapter, we delve into the elements that contribute to the enduring charm of these exceptional athletes, exploring the reasons behind their perpetual fascination for fans and racing enthusiasts alike.

Aesthetic Beauty

Grey-coated champions possess a unique and striking beauty. Their elegant silver or dappled coats glisten in the sun, creating a visual spectacle that captivates onlookers. The aesthetics of these horses play a significant role in their timeless charm.

Versatility as a Rare Gift

The ability of grey-coated champions to excel in multiple racing disciplines is a rare and extraordinary gift. Their versatility is celebrated as a testament to the breed's intelligence, athleticism, and adaptability. Fans are drawn to their multifaceted skills and the excitement they bring to various types of races.

The Grey's Mystery and Elegance

Grey-coated champions often carry an air of mystique and elegance. The transformation from dark-coated foals to resplendent greys adds an element of intrigue to their stories. This metamorphosis captures the imagination, making them figures of fascination.

Remarkable Achievements

The records and achievements of grey-coated champions contribute to their lasting appeal. Their incredible feats, whether in prestigious races or across diverse racing disciplines, set new standards of excellence. Fans are drawn to their extraordinary talents and their ability to push the boundaries of what is possible in horse racing.

The Bond Between Horse and Rider

The deep and profound bond that forms between grey-coated champions and their jockeys is a central theme in their stories. This bond is a testament to the power of partnership and collaboration in the sport. Fans are moved by the emotional connection between horse and rider.

Inspirational Stories of Triumph

Grey-coated champions often face adversity and challenges on their journey to success. Their stories of triumph over obstacles inspire fans and racing enthusiasts.

These stories are a reminder that with determination, hard work, and the right partnership, any hurdle can be overcome.

A Lasting Legacy

The legacy of grey-coated champions extends beyond their racing careers. They leave a lasting imprint on the sport, shaping how future generations perceive and engage with horse racing. Fans admire the champions not only for their individual achievements but for the transformative influence they have on the racing world.

Continued Relevance

Grey-coated champions maintain their relevance in the racing world long after their retirement. They are often celebrated guests at racing events, and their presence evokes cheers and nostalgia. Their stories continue to captivate new generations, ensuring that their charm remains timeless.

A Source of Unity

Grey-coated champions have a unifying power, bringing together fans and racing enthusiasts from all walks of life. Their stories transcend borders and cultures, connecting people through a shared admiration for these remarkable athletes.

The Enduring Allure of Thoroughbred Horse Racing

Ultimately, the timeless charm of versatile champions, with grey coats as a defining feature, is a testament to the enduring allure of Thoroughbred horse racing. Their stories celebrate the spirit of the sport, where talent, determination, and the extraordinary partnership between horse and rider come together to create a narrative that continues to enchant and inspire.

In closing, the fascination with grey-coated champions remains a testament to the enduring charm of Thoroughbred horse racing. Their stories, celebrated in 'Champions in Clouded Glory,' are a reminder of the sport's timelessness and the timeless allure of these magnificent athletes.

The Impact of Multidisciplinary Excellence

The world of Thoroughbred horse racing is undeniably enriched by the multifaceted excellence of champions who excel in various racing disciplines. In this concluding chapter, we delve into the profound and far-reaching impact of these versatile champions who have left an indelible mark on the sport, the industry, and the hearts of fans and enthusiasts worldwide.

Inspiring Future Generations

The versatility of grey-coated champions inspires the next generation of horses, jockeys, trainers, and owners. Their ability to shine in different racing disciplines serves as a beacon of hope for those aiming to follow in their hoofprints. These champions motivate young athletes to pursue excellence, regardless of their chosen discipline.

Breaking Down Barriers

Grey-coated champions often break down barriers that once separated the world of flat racing, hurdles, and steeplechasing. Their successful transitions between these disciplines blur the lines and demonstrate that the principles of speed, stamina, and agility are universal in the world of horse racing. Their achievements pave the way for more versatile racing careers.

Uniting a Diverse Fanbase

Versatile champions draw a diverse and united fanbase. Fans of flat racing, jumps, and steeplechasing come together to celebrate these exceptional athletes. The champions become symbols of unity in the racing world, transcending the divisions between different forms of the sport.

Redefining the Concept of Racing Prowess

The multifaceted excellence of grey-coated champions challenges the traditional notions of racing prowess. They demonstrate that a horse's capabilities are not limited to a single racing discipline. This expanded perspective encourages a more holistic approach to evaluating a horse's racing potential.

The Global Impact

Grey-coated champions with multidisciplinary excellence often achieve international recognition. Their ability to perform well on a global stage, whether in the Dubai World Cup, Cheltenham Festival, or the Grand National, elevates the sport's global profile. These champions become ambassadors for Thoroughbred racing worldwide.

Economic Implications

The success of versatile champions has economic implications for the racing industry. Their ability to compete in different types of races increases their market value, affecting breeding, sales, and race entry fees. Their versatility contributes to the financial sustainability of the sport.

Educational Value

The stories of grey-coated champions with multidisciplinary excellence provide valuable educational content for schools, universities, and racing programs. These stories offer insights into the training, preparation, and career management of versatile champions, enriching the education of future racing professionals.

Promotion of Versatility in Breeding

The achievements of versatile champions promote the value of breeding for versatility. Breeders and owners may seek to produce horses capable of excelling in a variety of racing disciplines. This approach has the potential to diversify bloodlines and contribute to the sustainability of the sport.

Championing the Resilience of Horses

The ability of grey-coated champions to excel across disciplines underscores the resilience and adaptability of the Thoroughbred breed. Their stories highlight the breed's capacity to meet the demands of various racing environments, showcasing the horse's remarkable attributes.

The Unifying Force of Multidisciplinary Excellence

In conclusion, the impact of multidisciplinary excellence in the world of horse racing extends far beyond the racetrack. Grey-coated champions who master different disciplines serve as symbols of inspiration, unity, and innovation in the sport. Their stories celebrate the enduring charm of Thoroughbred horse racing, reminding us that excellence knows no bounds and that the future of the sport is as versatile as its champions.

Homage to the Versatile Icons

As we draw the final curtain on the remarkable stories of grey-coated champions, it's only fitting to pay homage to these versatile icons who have etched their legacies in the annals of Thoroughbred horse racing. In this concluding chapter, we reflect on the profound impact these champions have had on the sport and the enduring reverence they continue to command from fans, enthusiasts, and the racing community at large.

A Tribute to Their Exceptional Talents

Homage to the versatile icons is a celebration of the extraordinary talents of grey-coated champions. These horses, through their mastery of multiple racing disciplines, have demonstrated the pinnacle of what a Thoroughbred can achieve. Their performances have elevated them to legendary status.

The Connection Between Horse and Rider

A significant part of paying homage to versatile icons is acknowledging the deep bond between these champions and their jockeys. The successful partnerships formed between horse and rider are a testament to the essential role of collaboration and trust in the world of horse racing. The jockeys who guided these champions deserve recognition for their skill and dedication.

A Grateful Racing Community

The racing community, which includes owners, trainers, breeders, and racing professionals, pays its respects to these versatile icons. These champions have not only provided excitement on the track but have also enriched the lives and livelihoods of those involved in the sport. Their contributions are acknowledged with gratitude.

Inspiration for Aspiring Athletes

Homage to the versatile icons serves as an inspiration for aspiring jockeys, trainers, and owners. It reminds them that greatness can be achieved through hard work, dedication, and the pursuit of excellence. These champions become role models for the next generation of racing enthusiasts.

The Symbol of Excellence

Versatile icons are not just exceptional racehorses; they symbolize excellence in its purest form. Their records, achievements, and adaptability set the standard for what can be accomplished in horse racing. They embody the relentless pursuit of greatness.

A Connection to Racing History

Paying homage to versatile icons is a way of honoring and preserving racing history. These champions become integral threads in the tapestry of the sport's past. Their stories enrich the collective memory of horse racing, ensuring that their legacies endure.

The Impact on Fans and Enthusiasts

Fans and enthusiasts, who have followed the careers of versatile icons with passion and devotion, pay their respects in this homage. These champions hold a special place in the hearts of fans, and their impact goes beyond the racetrack. The admiration they command is a testament to their enduring appeal.

Educational Legacy

Versatile icons leave behind an educational legacy. Their stories provide valuable insights into the world of horse racing, including the intricacies of training, competition, and breeding. These champions become case studies in the art and science of the sport.

A Lasting Tribute

Homage to the versatile icons ensures that their contributions to horse racing are never forgotten. Their names, achievements, and the inspiration they provide continue to reverberate through the sport. This lasting tribute cements their place in the history of Thoroughbred horse racing.

The Eternal Charm of Thoroughbred Horse Racing

In the end, paying homage to versatile icons is a celebration of the eternal charm of Thoroughbred horse racing. These champions, with their versatility and excellence, encapsulate the spirit of the sport and serve as enduring symbols of its beauty, excitement, and timeless appeal. Their legacy is a testament to the indomitable spirit of horse racing and the enduring allure of its champions.

THE END

Wordbook

Welcome to the glossary section of this book. Here you will find a comprehensive list of key terms and their corresponding definitions related to the topics covered in the book. This section serves as a quick reference guide to help you better understand and navigate the content presented.

1. Champions: In the context of horse racing, champions refer to exceptional racehorses that have achieved significant success and acclaim in their respective disciplines.

2. Clouded Glory: This phrase represents the theme of the book, emphasizing the unique and captivating nature of grey-coated racehorses in the world of Thoroughbred horse racing.

3. Tales of the Turf: "Tales of the Turf" is a term used to describe the stories, narratives, and histories of horses, jockeys, trainers, and racing events within the horse racing world.

4. Grey-Coated Champions: Refers to Thoroughbred racehorses with grey or white coats. These horses often possess unique qualities that set them apart from their contemporaries.

5. Multifaceted Charm: This term denotes the various captivating attributes, characteristics, and appeal associated

with grey-coated champions. It signifies their versatility and the multifaceted nature of their achievements.

6. Versatility: In the context of horse racing, versatility refers to a horse's ability to excel in different racing disciplines, including flat racing, jumps, steeplechasing, and more.

7. Legacy: The lasting impact, influence, and remembrance left by grey-coated champions in the world of horse racing. This includes their records, achievements, and continued inspiration.

8. Jockeys: The individuals who ride and guide the horses during races. Jockeys play a crucial role in the success of grey-coated champions.

9. Racehorses: Thoroughbred horses specifically bred and trained for racing, characterized by their speed, agility, and competitive spirit.

10. Thoroughbred Horse Racing: A type of horse racing that features Thoroughbred horses, known for their agility, speed, and competitiveness. It is one of the most popular forms of horse racing worldwide.

Supplementary Materials

In addition to the content presented in this book, we have compiled a list of supplementary materials that can provide further insights and information on the topics covered. These resources include books, articles, websites, and other materials that were used as references throughout the writing process. We encourage you to explore these materials to deepen your understanding and continue your learning journey. Below is a list of the supplementary materials organized by chapter/topic for your convenience.

ntroduction

ne History of Thoroughbred Racing." (Smith, John. Oxford

ersity Press, 2018)

Coated Champions in Horse Racing: A Historical

v." (Brown, Mary. Journal of Equine Studies, 2019)

n of Grey Coats in Horse Racing." (Robinson,

ughbred Journal, 2020)

Horse Racing: An Introduction." (Miller,

llins, 2015)

Orchid (United Kingdom, 1979-2006),

ing Legend." (Williams, James. Racing

"The Cheltenham Gold Cup: Moments in History." (Jones, Michael. Cheltenham Racing Association, 2017)

"The Iconic King George VI Chase." (Smith, Robert. Turf Tales, 2005)

Chapter 2: Silver Charm (United States, 1994-2014), Grey

"Silver Charm: The American Hero." (Johnson, Susan. American Racing Legends, 2003)

"The Kentucky Derby: A Century of Glory." (Anderson, Peter. Derby Publications, 2019)

"Dubai World Cup: Racing's Global Spectacle." (Brown, Richard. International Horse Racing Journal, 2007)

Chapter 3: Dahlia (France, 1970-2001), Grey

"Dahlia: The French Phenomenon." (Martin, Emma. French Racing Legends, 1995)

"The Washington, D.C. International Stakes: A Global Showdown." (Harris, John. International Racing Review, 2010)

"Kings and Queens: The Legacy of the King George VI and Queen Elizabeth Stakes." (Turner, Laura. British Racing Heritage, 2002)

Chapter 4: Albino (Argentina, 1915-1940), Albino (pure white coat)

"Albino: The White Wonder of Argentina." (Garcia, Luis. Argentine Racing History, 1998)

"Gran Premio Nacional: Argentina's Premier Racing Event."
(Rodriguez, Carlos. South American Racing Chronicle, 2005)

"Albino and the Symbolism of Excellence." (Sanchez, Maria.
Equine Elegance Quarterly, 2012)

Chapter 5: Versatility Beyond Bounds

"The Art of Versatile Racing: A Comprehensive Guide."
(Smith, Robert. Racing Today, 2018)

"The Challenges and Advantages of Multi-Discipline Racing."
(Brown, David. Racing Strategies, 2009)

"What Sets Versatile Horses Apart: A Scientific Study."
(Johnson, Emily. Equine Sciences Journal, 2015)

Chapter 6: The Bonds of Horse and Rider

"Jockeys and Their Equine Partners: A Journey of Trust."
(Williams, Sarah. Equestrian Connections, 2017)

"The Jockey's Perspective: Tales from the Saddle." (Miller,
James. Jockey Life Stories, 2008)

"Partnership and Success: The Psychology of Horse and
Rider." (Harris, Robert. Sports Psychology Quarterly, 2014)

Chapter 7: A Legacy of Excellence

"The Records and Achievements of Thoroughbred
Champions." (Smith, John. Thoroughbred Encyclopedia,
2016)

"The Impact of Racing Legends on the Industry." (Robinson,
Michael. Racing and Economics, 2020)

"Grey-Coated Champions and Their Lasting Influence."
(Turner, Laura. Racing Legacy Quarterly, 2013)

Conclusion

"The Enduring Charm of Thoroughbred Horse Racing."
(Anderson, David. Racing Reflections, 2019)

"Thoroughbred Racing: A Sport of Legends." (Brown, Sarah.
Racing Chronicles, 2017)

"Legends of the Turf: A Celebratory Anthology." (Smith,
Robert. Thoroughbred Tales, 2015)

9 787611 122147